Acknowledgem

I would like to thank all my family for their support and encouragement in writing this book. Thanks in particular to my daughter Alison for editing and bringing this work to print, and to Cathy's cousin, Monica, for her help and boundless enthusiasm.

Enjoying this collection?
See David's other publications (available on Amazon):

Deals of a Lifetime: The true adventures of an antiques dealer over seven decades

by David John Claude Roper

Poems To Refresh The Soul

by Mr David Roper

RHYMES AND REASON

INTRODUCTION

This collection of poems, like my first book, "Poems to Refresh the Soul", is a reflection of the period of grief which most of us will experience at some time in our lives. In my case, it was the loss of my dearest wife Catherine (Cathy) in 2022, almost 3 years ago. At the time, an acquaintance of mine, who had lost his wife almost 20 years before, at the very young age of 39, said to me, "I would like to say it gets easier with time, but it doesn't". I can say now that he was absolutely right, it doesn't, and others in similar circumstances have confirmed this to be so. However, that is not to say that we should be gloomy all the time, our loved ones would not want that, grief, after all is a reflection of a great love which we were fortunate enough to have had and shared during our lifetime. I have tried to illustrate this in the poem "What is Grief" contained in this latest book,and an understanding of not feeling better with time is, hopefully, conveyed in another poem entitled "I Would Like To Say." The poem entitled "Big Coloured Bird" was inspired by a friend of my late father, who, when I went to tell her that he had passed, just a few hours later, she knew, as around that exact time she had seen what she described as "a bird of magnificent colours" in a tree in her garden, (which my father had tended for her), she said it was like nothing she had ever seen. She was sure it was my father letting her know that he had departed.

As before, I have endeavoured to show we can have lighter moments, in which we recognise something which our loved ones would have found amusing, been indignant about, or perhaps remembering a romantic moment we had shared with them.

In this latest collection of mine, I hope you will find something you recognise, as you continue your journey through life without that special someone you loved, a "rhyme and a reason."

NOT TODAY

I shed a tear or two
For you today,
Not the first,
I have to say.
I wonder if this pain
Is here forever,
Here to stay,
Will it ever go away?
I think it might,
But not today.

I shed a tear again today
I went to visit,
Where in peace you lay,
In the cold East wind's shrill,
I stood and cried
In the early morning chill,
And missed you.
Will this pain not go away?
Maybe it might,
But not today.

I shed a tear or two
As there I stood,
And wondered more,
And to touch, if I could,
Your hand to feel,
Perhaps a kiss to steal,
Still this pain it does not cease,
But still I hope
You rest in peace.

I shed a tear again today,
Will this pain
Not go away?
They say it will,
But not today!

MILLIONS

A million little raindrops,
A million light years in the sky,
Millions, yes and many more,
But only one of you and I.

A trillion little ice drops,
As many leaves blow by,
More stars than you can count,
But only one of you and I.

More grains of sand in the desert
That get into your eye,
More than you could ever count,
But, only one of you and I.

Millions yes, and millions more
Will be born, and then will die,
Millions of teardrops to be shed,
But only one, for you and I.

A BIRTHDAY REMEMBERED

If I counted all the raindrops
That fell down from on high,
Or counted all the stars
That brighten up the sky,
Still they wouldn't add up
To the tears that I have shed,
Since I looked upon the pillow
Where once you laid your head.

If I counted all the sand
That lies along the shore,
Or counted all the fish that swim
The ocean, to explore.
If I counted all the starlings
As in the sky they flew,
It wouldn't equal all the pain
That I felt for the loss of you.

If I counted all the clouds
That drift across the sky,
Or counted all the leaves
That in autumn blow on by,
Or counted every grain
That grows in that cornfield,
It wouldn't equal all the pain
That each birthday has revealed.

SAILING

The sun sets on another day
A day that has been blessed,
Life is what we make it,
We must just try our best.

To be upbeat and keep smiling
Is not an easy thing,
Bouncing back when trodden down,
With the pain that it can bring.

Set sail into the sunset
Midst hope and some good cheer,
Sail along the coast line
Remember who you're near.

THE HOUSE

The house is just a home,
A place for two to share,
A place within existence,
To help each other care.

This house is just so empty,
Without you here to dwell,
The days and nights just merging,
The difference, hard to tell.

No matter now what happens,
Of love that isn't spoken,
Nothing defines the emptiness,
Now the spell is broken.

The silence and the stillness
Brings in a sombre morn,
Invisible clouds of sorrow,
Drier than a desert storm.

ASK A SILLY QUESTION

The parrot asked the jackdaw,
Tell me, what's your name?
The jackdaw wouldn't answer,
He thought it was a game.

Tell me asked the donkey,
Why do they call me an ass?
Not a clue, replied the pony
You're just second class.

Tell me, asked the fox,
As out his liar he crept,
Where have all the hennies gone?
I must have overslept!

Tell me, asked the squirrel,
As he climbed a tree,
What makes you think I'm stupid?
I bet you can't catch me!

Tell me, asked the rabbit,
Unto his neighbour hare,
Why do you run so very fast,
When you've no idea to where?

Tell me, asked the blackbird,
Of a friendly crow,
What's your favourite, worm or slug?
The crow replied, I'll let you know.

Tell me, asked the werewolf,
Unto his friend the skelly,
Why don't you make more noise?
Give your voice some welly!

Tell me, asked the meerkat,
Of Carl, the helpful wombat,
How do I stop this leak?
Said he, use a rubber grommet!

Tell me asked the snowman,
Is it hot in here?
Better take your hat off,
That'll make it clear.

Tell me, asked the elephant
Why do camels have a hump?
Do behave, replied the camel.
Go and pack your trunk.

Tell me, asked the duck,
To the colourful drake,
Why are you so pretty?
Just swimming around the lake.

The drake replied, haughtily,
If I, like you, were plain,
They'd pull the plug on the lake,
And we'd all go down the drain.

So, ask a silly question,
And the answer you might get
Is not what you expected,
You'll think twice next time, I bet.

A HALO AROUND HELL

For some poor souls, life is tough
The masters in their existence,
Will try to justify the pain,
No matter how they present it,
Was for their greedy gain.

No matter how they twist it,
Or the lies that they can tell,
No matter what persuasion,
You can't put a halo around hell.

Dedicated to all victims of persecution and violence.

TWENTY FOUR MONTHS

Where are you today, my love?
Amongst the planets and the stars,
Where have you travelled to,
In this universe so vast?
Are you looking down on us
Has the spell been cast?

I wonder how far you've gone,
I wonder if you know
That here, in this sad old world,
We all miss you so,
Your warmth and smile are missing,
They made each day to glow.

The spirit it can travel,
Through centuries of time,
Light years and dominions,
Galaxies as yet unseen,
Stars in their trillions,
In light we've never seen.

We are sad and miss you,
But that may not be right,
We forget you have your freedom,
To rest in pure delight,
With all the spirits that are calm,
And bask in heaven's light.

I WOULD LIKE TO SAY….

I'd like to say I feel much better,
But I don't,
So I can't,
And I won't.

I'd like to say time is a healer,
But it's not,
So I can't,
And I won't.

I'd like to say that I don't miss you,
But I do,
So I can't,
And I won't.

I'd like to say that life's normal,
But it;s not,
So I can't,
And I won't.

I'd like to say that I'm coping,
But I'm not,
So I can't,
And I won't.

I'd like to say that for others,
I know that they understand,
But they don't,
So I can't,
And I won't.

I'd like to say I'm optimistic,
But I'm not,
So I can't,
And I won't.

I'd like to say, rest in peace,
Wherever you are meant now to be,
And I do,
So I will,
AND I DID

DANCE

Dance with me, if you will,
Around the stars of heaven,
Along the passageways of time,
Up and down the corridors,
With the love that's yours and mine.

Dance with me, if you will,
With hands that intertwine,
Round and round the maypole
Together keeping time,
With your love, and mine.

Dance with me, if you will,
Up and down the sunbeams,
Holding on so tight,
Hoping I can keep you,
Forever, in my sight.

COLOUR

All the colour left my world,
Just a dark grey hue,
That's all there is remaining
Since the day that I lost you.

The bright colours of the rainbow,
Red, yellow, orange and blue,
Left the stage when you bowed out,
All brightness went with you.

WALKING

Walk in the woods with me,
Take me by the hand,
Walk in the woods my love
Help me understand.

Walk in the woods my love,
Where we have been before,
Walk in the woods with me,
With love for evermore.

Walk in the woods with me,
The trees so bold and tall,
Walk in the woods my love,
Engrossed in deep love's call.

Walk in the woods my love,
With sunshine and no rain,
Walk once more through the woods
Together once again.

Come back and walk with me,
Walk in the woods again,
Although you had to leave me,
That's surely heaven's gain.

WHAT IS GRIEF

What is grief
If it is not love
Transformed inside your heart?
What is grief
If it is not love
That's torn your soul apart.

What is grief
But different love,
That burns both deep and bright.
What is grief
If it is not love
That keeps you in my sight?.

What is grief
But hidden love,
That burns through night and day,
What is grief
That makes it tough
Now you've gone away?.

What is grief
If it is not love,
That's somehow lost its way?
What is grief
If I cannot speak
Of missing you each day?

LOVE, A FOUR LETTER WORD

Love, is a four letter word,
Love is kind,
Love is care,
Love is good,
More than just a four letter word.

Love, it knows not hate,
True love is always fair,
Love is more than just a bond,
Love, it spells out share.

Love knows not envy,
Love is full of grace,
Love knows no pain,
Leaves no vacant space.

EVENING TIME

When the sun goes in
And hides its face,
Beneath the nighttime sky.
The stars appear,
The moon pops out,
And clouds go rolling by.

When day is done,
And goes to sleep,
Beneath the dusky sky,
May all the world
Rest in peace,
Within its closing eye.

GOLDEN SPIRIT

May golden spirits
Light your day,
And all that's good
Come down your way.

May the spirits
Burning bright,
Illuminate your soul,
Through day and night.

WITHIN THE MIRROR

When I gaze into the mirror,
Nothing can I see,
Nothing in the reflection,
That isn't just of me.
Not even just a shadow,
Of someone who I knew,
Someone that I cared for,
And miss each day anew.

In the mirror when I look,
I don't see you at all,
Not in spirit nor in flesh,
Until I am aware,
A tingling of the senses
Telling me you're there,
And that you're listening,
And for me still care.

BLESSE'D

Blesse`d are the memories
That I have each day of you,
Blesse`d all the memories,
That often I review.

Time spent together when
Life could bring distress,
But always joined together,
Life became success.

Joy in every sunset,
And happiness together shared.
Yes, blesse`d are the memories
Of life, enriched with care.

ANGELS WINGS

I have had a vision,
Of an angel's wings,
Soft, white, and gleaming,
Smooth as any silk,
Drifting down so gently,
Silent and serene,
Could it be I'm dreaming,
Or is this heaven's queen?

I have this lovely vision
Quite often now it seems,
Folds of soft white feathers,
Laid out like a heart,
Appearing out of nowhere,
Hovering, still and silent,
Arms stretched out in prayer.

Angels wings of purest white
Elegant as lace,
Fills the room with magic
On an air of silent grace.
Magnificent and calming,
A comfort to my soul,
Angel wings from heaven,
Must surely be our goal.

DAILY FINDS

Just a daily, routine thing
Can trigger such a blow,
Looking for an address
Inside the book you kept,
And there in your own hand
A number, and a name,
Of someone that you knew
Who was always glad to hear
From you....

In that very familiar hand,
Which I recognised at once,
Such memories are ignited,
As sadness claims the day.
Memories, now in the past,
Seeming distant, far away,
But in a way, they are good,
That's all there is to say.

But then, another blow
I see a late addition
That you wrote when ill,
The neat and careful writing,
Gives way to shaky, stumbling,
Which you tried hard to conceal,
Much pain, and some distress,
As with difficulty you struggled,
To record a new address.

THE COTTAGE

I have a picture in my mind
Of a little cottage,
Perched upon a hill,
Roses growing round the door,
And you are with me still.

I have a picture which I see,
Of a pretty garden bench
Shaded by a tree,
Basking in the sunlight,
And you're sitting there with me.

I wonder is this heaven
This picture which I see?
Just sitting in the sunshine
Relaxed, devoid of care,
And you beside, with me.

BLACK DAY THOUGHTS

Life is cold without you,
Each day seems relentless,
Little comfort to daily life,
What is the point I wonder,
Without my lovely wife?
My constant life companion,
In every waking breath,
In hollow contemplation,
Now lost in blackest death.
What is the point, I wonder?
I struggle just to talk,
I cannot find a reason,
To take a daily walk.

I know I should be grateful
With the things that I do have,
But I feel somehow lost,
In days of darkest gloom,
Sometime we all must face it,
Death just comes too soon.
I'm lucky that I had you,
And the time together shared,
Days, they come and go,
An epitaph of reason
We must just shrug and bear,
Everyone who loved someone
Knows to value care.

LOST IN MYSTERY

All is lost
In the mystery of time
Nothing found,
Nothing seen,
All lost in the mystery of time.

All is lost
We worry and we fret,
Nothing gained
Nothing yet
Evades the mystery of time.

Is all lost?
Who knows if that is so,
Who can tell
If we can
Evade the mystery of time..

Is it so?
We may never know
If it's true,
If we do
It's hidden, in the mystery of time.

GRAVEYARD VISIT

I walked to the graveyard today
To visit those laid at rest,
I saw two sad old men
Shuffling, both looked lost.
I was moved to pity them,
Then I realised, of course,
There were in fact, three sad souls
With me, who looked the same.

That scene must be repeated,
Every day, with others just as we,
Who come along to reminisce,
And mourn, along with me,
All looking sad, dejected,
Lost and waiting yet,
For the call to join you,
Resting, lest we forget.

DOOR OF DEATH

Do not fear the door
Which we must all pass through,
The exit not clearly marked
For all, no matter who.

You can't evade this door
Or death's cold chilly hand,
It is the only exit
To leave this familiar land.

The brightest rays of sunshine
Are on the other side,
So do not fear the door
From which you cannot hide.

PILGRIMS

Many are my friends,
Sadly now departed,
Lifted from this earthly coil,
Leaving loved ones broken hearted.

Pilgrims of our time,
Along life's bumpy track,
Searching forward, off they went,
For them, no going back.

Pilgrims of our time,
Exploring, they were sent
Many wonders to behold,
And ponder what it meant.

A VISITATION

Like it or not
One day we will die,
Our breath it will stop
And bodies will rot,
So the spirit escapes,
Once more to be free,
To visit us mortals,
But them, we won't see.

A spirit can't be heard
And seldom is seen,
But will leave traces,
To show that they've been,
A feather, a cushion
Just moved out of place,
A matter of presence,
But of them, not a trace.

A book left open at
A place that you know,
Or a pen dropped beside
The chair where they sat.
You'll see the sign
Carefully left there,
The spirit will have called
To show that they still care.

CLOUDS

Bring in the clouds
That herald the rain,
It's that time of year
That's come here again.

The clouds that surround
The sky as we look,
Much better at calming
Than reading a book.

The clouds of white
And sometimes of grey
Drift slowly by,
Throughout every day.

Fluffy, soft as wool
Moving steady we see,
An invisible pull
Like sand, near the sea.

AUTUMN OF LIFE

The gently swirling autumn breeze
Disturbs the lightly browning leaves,
Changing the skyline, green into brown,
Watch the leaves float gently down,
Just like we, they are dying
Their job is done, it's mesmerising.
It's the cycle of birth and of death,
Rushing now, toward their rest.

The clouds and skyline are a-changing
We view the horizon re-arranging,
Just to see that time is pressing,
Days grow shorter and light is fading,
Shadows from the sun now shading.
A different world becomes the view,
Surely we must follow too,
But come the spring, all will renew.

THINK OF ME

Wherever you go,
Think always of me,
Who loved you so dearly,
And I know, you loved me.

Wherever you go
Carry no doubt,
That I shall be there
As you wonder about.

So wherever it is
Think only of me
I could be just there,
Under that tree.

BIG COLOURED BIRD

There's a big coloured bird
Of magnificent hue,
That inhabits the sky
Mostly hidden from view.

This bird it appears
To show signs of peace,
That in spite of a loss,
Love does not cease.

It's comforting to see,
Such a thing of good grace,
Transporting our pain
From this earthly space.

So look for this bird
As a soul wends its way,
To remind us of someone
Who surrendered this day.

Inspired following the death of my Father, and a vision seen by a friend.

BLACK HOLE

What is it I wonder?
That digs this big black hole,
Which often near engulfs me,
My poor and lonely soul.

What is it I wonder?
That pulls upon my heart,
Making me feel as if
It's tearing me apart.

I can bear it no more,
Tell it please do stop,
Like drowning in teardrops,
From bottom to the top.

This deep black hole grows daily,
At an alarming rate,
Someone, stop it please,
Before it is too late.

SLEEPLESS

I lie awake, at this ungodly hour,
Listening to the raindrops,
In another heavy shower,
Not able to sleep, restless
I toss and I turn, get up every hour,
My mind is still active, no peace,
I turn on the radio, no power,
So try to forget what I'm thinking,
Shutting my eyes, try sleep once again,
Turnover to think, but no good,
I'm starting to think I'm insane.

SUITCASE AND SILK

The suitcase may be battered,
Well used and maybe torn,
But the silken gown within it
Is shiny, scarcely worn.

Like the battered suitcase,
With body black and blue,
Bruised and maybe crumbling,
But your spirit is as new.

Protect that gown of silk,
Within the case well used,
Pray to help the spirit,
In a body hurt and bruised.

The inspiration for this came from the trauma experienced by a dear friend following several falls.

MIDNIGHT MOONLIGHT

Meet me by the broken bridge,
At half past midnight,
Surrounded just by nature
In the pale moonlight.

Meet me by the crooked tree,
At half past midnight,
In the eerie silence,
Of cool celestial light.

Meet me neath the winter moon,
Just below the ridge,
Come hold me in the dark,
By the broken bridge.

At half past midnight,
In a setting so serene,
Together we will pledge our love,
In a magic moonlight scene.

NEW DAY

Over the valley,
Out on the hills,
The new day sunshine,
Breaks up the clouds,
Slowly shining through them,
As outwardly, it spills.

New day breaks,
Upon the hills serene,
Bringing fresh hope
And opportunity.
Search and you will find it,
In a setting cool and green.

A new day dawns,
Slumper yawns,
Effort is needed
Ideas to be heeded.
Best get started,
Tomorrow is,
Already here..!

WONDERING SOUL

Three in the morning, sleepless,
Beneath a bright full moon,
My soul, no place to go,
Just tossing and a'turning
Like waiting for grass to grow.

Four in the morning, now
Still tossing and a'turning,
And thinking what to do,
Always I will turn,
To thinking, just of you.

Five in the morning, now
So I start to wonder,
As tomorrow shines its ray,
Will I still remember,
What I did today?

OLD MAN IN THE PARK

A sad old man is sitting,
On a bench beside the gate,
Looking very pensive,
As life he contemplates.

He looks at busy people,
Running through the park,
As the sun is setting,
Soon, it will be dark.

The day was nearly over,
And no one had he seen,
So he came into the park,
To sit amongst the green.

No one to speak to,
No one to say hello,
Might as well be invisible,
Slowly he gets up to go.

"What's your name mister?"
Said a voice from down below,
A little girl is standing, smiling,
At an old man she didn't know.

"My name is Ellie, what's yours?"
He starts to reply to say,
When her mother grabs her hand,
"Don't bother the man that way"

"It really is no bother,"
He answered with a smile,
She's the only one who's spoken,
And I've been here..quite a while.

"Well we must be leaving"
The mother stared ahead,
Then, with some hesitation,
These words to him she said.

"I know you, you're Albert
I thought that you were....dead"
"Not yet" he smiled at her discomfort,
As she realized what she'd said.

They walked together to the gate,
Into the sun's last ray,
It was just a little girl,
Who made an old man's day.

He went there often after,
To watch the children play,
They are life's innocents,
Who know just what to say.

They have no inhibitions,
Bringing happiness your way,
So always smile, and say, hello,
And make somebody's day.

FORCE OF EVIL

Evil is a wicked thing
It finds the weakness in us all,
Penetrates the human soul,
Expands into a monster
And slowly, takes control.

But love is the greater weapon
If mixed with gentleness,
Will overcome the evil one,
And all his emptiness.

So bring forward compassion,
Generosity, and good grace,
And always look at human love
With a smile upon your face.

Down into the darkest depths
Of human cruelty,
Look to give, and give again
To all that are in need,
Turn away all selfish thoughts,
Expel all human greed.

THE NICE WITCH

There is an ole' witch
Who lives in a ditch,
No cat, cauldron or broom.
You might think,
What a silly witch
To inhabit a ditch,
And wonder,
Where does she sleep?
But as we discovered,
The ditch it is covered
In moss, twigs, and old leaves.

So, lift up a twig
Look well beneath,
Just to see, is she there?
She won't mind a bit
If there she just sits,
Looking demure and serene,
Because, this old witch,
Who lives in the ditch
Is kind, and not at all mean.

So, when in the woods,
Behave like you should,
And don't make a mess
Or cause any stress,
To those that within it do dwell,
Like the witch in the ditch,
Who seldom will cast a bad spell.

Make no mistake, if you do
That mistake you will rue,
For, if her sister's about,
She'll surely come out,
And turn you into a shrew!

OBI THE CAT

We once had a cat called Obi,
Fluffy, grey and white.
He stayed out all night,
To hunt out a rat
As big as the cat,
And brought it home as a trophy.

Now what a loyal cat
Each night to catch a rat,
Sometimes more than just one.
Till one night he met his match,
Was hit by a car as, triumphantly
He headed home with his catch.

The vet was aghast when she looked,
As for an X ray he was booked,
She submitted a bill
That made me feel ill,
But I paid the big whack, so
Once mended, Obi came back.

Obi returned home to live,
And happily continued to give
His best, for us every day.
In retirement he played
But at night, out he stayed,
And still came home with a trophy.

NOVEMBER

I wonder, will I return
To this place, different time,
I wonder, could it just be
If November again I shall see?

The place which I remember
In the last November,
Seems very familiar,
Not at all dissimilar.

Could it just be,
That maybe I'll see,
When it comes round again,
Just another November!

November precedes December,
As another month, it passes,
I wonder, does it seem better,
If viewed through rose tinted glasses?

NATURE IN AUTUMN

As the wind gently rustles,
Through autumn browning leaves,
Now loosened from the trees,
Down to the ground they flutter,
Covering the grass,
And filling the gutter.

Nature quietly busy
Doing what must be done,
As autumn mists
Replace the sun.
So begin the winter sneezes
As beneath our feet, it freezes.

Midnight comes, then it goes,
In the silence of night it snows.
Thus nature works
While we all sleep,
The routine of seasons
It will keep.

WHAT AM I?

I am not seen
And seldom heard,
Not a man
Nor feathered bird.
I cannot see
Or yet be seen.
I'm not a king
Nor beauty queen.
Not of flesh
And bones am I.
No, I am not
Of these things,
Then to this life
What do I bring,
Since I cannot speak
And cannot sing?
I am a dancing shadow,
Inside moonbeams,
That gently mingle.
An unseen presence,
Whose silent movement,
Makes skin tingle.

ABSENCE

Life without you
Isn't life at all,
Like a house,
Built with a roof
But lacking any wall.

Life is very empty,
Often very bleak,
Hard to be positive,
Seems to get much harder
With each passing week.

You deserved much more
So I often think,
When things were tough,
You were there, with a hug,
And things got better, in a blink.

CHASING

I chase the night
To lose the day,
Will I ever
Find the way?

PEACE

If peace for all
Cannot be WON.
What er'e the cost
Then peace for all,
Must not be LOST.

MUSING

If you reach the morning,
You've survived.
If you reach the evening,
You've arrived.
If you reach happiness
You've succeeded!

MOONLIGHT

Moonlight shining brightly,
Houses silhouetted, silently,
Appearing to be frozen
In the frosty ground.

Moonlit shadows haunting,
The ear picks out no sound,
No owls a'screeching,
Just Mr fox, who is seeking
Supper to be found.

An exquisite scene to paint,
With nature to acquaint,
Stillness, with no sound.
A town just wrapped in silence
Within a shadowed gown.

Like a haunting melody,
But devoid of sound.
A ghostly place,
So pale of face,
It lies uncluttered
On the frozen ground.

ROSES IN MOONLIGHT

Moonlight and roses
A gift for all time,
Moonlight with roses
A gift so divine.

Moonlight with roses
A time not to miss,
Moonlight and roses
A heavenly kiss..

Moonlight and roses
No better could be,
Moonlight on roses,
A gift for eternity.

Moonlight and roses
A heavenly gift,
Flowers in moonlight
Will heal any rift.

Moonlight and romance
What better to be,
Embracing with true love,
For you and for me.

THE MIGHTY OAK

The oak tree stands
Proud and so tall,
Mighty and defiant,
Started as an acorn,
And grew into a giant.

King of the forest with
Timber stout and strong,
Built into great ships,
Exploring oceans vast,
Carrying men across the world,
Sails of canvas at the mast.

Thus mighty things
From acorns grow.
We are truly thankful,
To nature's woodland king,
For what to us is given
And the adventures it can bring.

HERE STILL

Your voice is heard
On the wind,
Through the weathered tree,
Everywhere your voice is heard,
So gently, calling me.

Your smile is ever present
In the morning sun,
As from slumber deep
I rise to greet the day,
A promise still to keep.

Your voice is heard
Over people that I meet
Whispering oh so gently.
Perhaps you are that stranger,
Passing in the street.

Your warmth is felt
Throughout each chilly day.
Your love is all embracing
As gently I'm reminded
It never went away.

CURIOSITY CABINET

Life is like a cabinet
To display and to preserve,
The richness and the fullness
Of all that we observe.
The beauty and the ugliness,
Of life which we collect,
From the splendour of heaven,
To the depths of darkest hell,
Whatever is the flavour
Be sure, display it well.

Within life's fleeting moments
Lie treasures we must keep,
Showing where we've been to,
Or things which make us weep.
Stored within life's cabinet,
Standing side by side,
The cabinet of curiosities,
Keeps our fondest memories
Very much alive..

JOY

Joy is in hands that touch,
An unspoken word,
That means so much.

Joy is in the silent glance,
Between two loves who met
Through destiny, not chance.

Joy is in each passing day,
That keeps on giving
More, along life's way.

Joy is in that loving look,
That tells a story , better
Than any romantic book.

Joy is in the knowing,
That love in destiny
Just keeps growing.

THE IRISH GIRL

On a visit to my aunt one day,
Evening time, during May,
So unexpected, so thrilling,
In a strange way, chilling,
Unexpected, undeserved,
For there, upon the chair
Sat a girl with lovely hair,
And lovely legs, I have to say.
I was blinded, blown away,
That was how I first met,
The lovely Irish girl.

Such lovely, jet black hair
And a smile that dazzled,
In that moment of emotion
My heart felt, frazzled.
This is my lodger, Kathleen
My Aunt explained.
But I wasn't listening
Just looking at the eyes
Smiling, glistening,
Not to mention all the rest!
The lovely Irish girl.

Next day I returned in haste,
With some excuse, or other,
Knowing there was no time to waste.
I asked, my voice all a quiver,
If she would like to see
The colleges, that back along the river,
Flowing through the city
With springtime flowers
And blossoms, pretty,
Though not as she,
The lovely Irish girl.

Seemed just a moment, when,
Without hesitation she replied
"Yes, I'd like that very much".
As into my car she seated
I felt her closeness,
My hesitations, thus defeated,
I felt emboldened
To ask her out once more,
When back at auntie's door,
And she said "yes"
My exciting, lovely Irish girl.

We started to date
More regularly then,
That's when I began,
Inspired, I took up the pen,
I wrote her a poem,
And then, another.
Soon she was hooked,
That I could see,
But couldn't believe,
That she'd fallen for me,
That lovely Irish girl.

I soon realised, no surprise
She was very popular at home,
With marriage proposals four,
Or perhaps, even more?
As I gazed into her eyes
I thought for me, no chance,
Not even a second glance
When I made it number five.
So when she answered yes,
I was ecstatic, you can guess,
My lovely Irish girl.

She inspired me so to write
Another poem every night,
She brought to me so much,
A warm and loving, gentle touch.
Love, with so much joy.
Our love contiued growing,
Smoothing out the bumps
That are life's journey,
It wasn't always easy
For my lovely Irish girl.

We took a flight across the sea
To the town that was her home,
Belfast, where she had her roots,
Before to England, she did roam.
There it was I met her folks,
And for them to see
What she'd brought home,
From across the sea,
A protestant, an Englishman
Who, now sort the hand,
Of this lovely Irish girl.

So, at last, the knot was tied
In August of that year,
Joining us to each together,
For fifty and six years,
With a family of six,
And a faith now shared.
Problems, they were little ones,
We for each other, so much cared,
Till she was called to go
To leave this earthly life,
My lovely Irish girl.

With passing time it does seem,
An eternity, a hideous dream
Since I lost my Irish girl.
She was a passing shadow
Within the links of time,
But to me, so much, a wife
A mother, confidant, a friend,
An inspiration, throughout life
Time just seemed a whirl,
Of contentment, and much love
With my lovely Irish girl.

DRIFTING

Silent spirit of the night
Bring to me dawn's new light,
Bring me to the waking hour
With all the joy,
Within your power.

Silent spirit, ghostly dreams,
Never being what it seems,
To gaze aloft at the stars,
Dreaming of a pilgrimage,
To visit Mars.

Whilst our earthly body sleeps,
Into our future, the soul it peeps,
Drifting outward, upward yonder,
To give a glimpse
Of that we ponder.

Heavens vast expanse out there,
Light years beyond our stare.
Moving swiftly, ever onward,
Through many stages,
Our imagination it engages.

SLEEP

As darkness falls
To close the day,
The hours of sleep
Outward reach,
To give respite,
In slumber deep.

Silently I dream
Of what is past,
A life that's been.
With you there,
Let me find again,
What death laid bare.

As the night
Transforms to day,
I dreamed once more
You came to stay.
I pray, when I wake,
My newfound joy
Dawn will not take.

HOURS OF DARK

Within seductive hours of dark,
Searching for some peace,
Visiting the land of dreams,
Where life, it does not cease.
I can find you in that place,
Of the little that I know,
A place of great mystery
Where in life, I cannot go.

Within the resting hours of dark
Lie emotions I'm aware
Where I know to find you,
Knowing that you're there.
In this place
I'm not forsaken,
So when sleep is done,
Daylight bids me waken.

Inside those relics of the past,
I long again, to hover,
But this visit is so brief
I scarcely know of time,
To find then some relief,
Come now, dawn is calling,
Say not farewell, or adieu,
I just want....the earthly you.

Within seductive hours of dark
I cannot dally long,
You are there, but I know
In life's short journey,
Which we shared,
There was love,
So, with gladness, I can see
You rest in heaven, blissfully.

TANGERINE SKIES

Tangerine skies, a word from the wise,
Mists rise, fools deride,
Blue lagoon, harvest moon.

Mists that fall, over all,
Fairies prance, all in a trance
Leading all a merry dance.

Trees so tall, as a wall,
On a mound, all around.
Lightning strikes, like flashing lights.

Tangerine skies, twinkling eyes
A wondrous scene, might have been,
Perhaps…a dream….!

A SOUL WEEPING

In a windswept graveyard
A soul is heard a-weeping,
Looking for a home
To inhabit for safekeeping.

A soul that lived a life
But was not loved,
Cannot rest in peace,
Lies instead, just weeping.

A refuge it is seeking
Love in human form,
No more a-weeping
And feeling so forlorn.

Kindness is essential
To find a lasting home,
No more to be a-weeping
A new body just to clone.

Escaping the graveyard
The soul, no longer bound.
A love for all eternity,
Peace at last is found.

WHAT, IF, AND HOW.

Come , great monument
To life and love,and all,
Come and rest a while
With me, yes,
And draw breath,
Inside the furrowed brow,
Come and rest, and tell to me,
What, if, and how?.

Come greet life's challenges
Occurring every day,
Come, explain to me,
Did you find a way?
Come, sit, and tell to me
I beg you please,
Now it's done,
What, if, and how?.

Come great monument
Of love, now please do tell,
What you have discovered,
Within that deep, dark well?.
Come and sit beside me,
Where we now do dwell,
And share with me,
What, if, and how?.

BIRD SONG

The sweetest sound I ever heard
Was from a little feathered bird,
As the early morning sun,
Brought the day along,
Dawn was welcomed,
As birds commenced their song.

Nothing like it in this world,
Could excel that little bird.
Then the others, they joined in,
All together, a heavenly din
Bidding us, arise
Welcome in the morning skies.

Come now, raise your head,
Don't just lie there a'bed
As when you are, thus so
You'll not hear the cock to crow,
So rise to the birdsong clear,
And hug your loved one dear.

COLD DARK NIGHT

When on a cold dark night
And to bed I go,
It seems uninviting,
Unwelcoming.
A cold dark place,
No smiling face,
Or frilly lace.
You are not there,
I feel despair.

A cold dark night
Filled with fright,
Your warm hand,
It is not there.
Who will care
That I cannot sleep,
And if I do,
I dream of you.

In this dark cold place,
Just sadness,
Lacking gladness
To warm the heart,
To bring content
Of happier times,
Once spent.

DO ANGELS STILL SING?

Do angels still sing in heaven?
Or do they weep to see,
The things that we are doing,
Because we think we're free.

Do angels sing in heaven?
Or weep for all humanity,
For the damage that's inflicted
With vengeance, and no humility.

Can angels sing in heaven?
With all that man has done,
Destroying all we were given
To protect us, every one.

Do angels still sing in heaven?
Or do they weep to see.
Do they sing a chorus,
In stars we cannot see.?

Do angels sing in heaven?
I hope they still will do,
And pray for our salvation,
Mistakes we'll surely rue.

WHAT IS THE POINT?

What's the point I ponder,
Of anything I do,
When everything lacks the touch
That only came with you.

What's the point of each task,
If it isn't done for you,
When the day isn't black,
It's a grisly kind of blue.

The point of everything
Is not for us to know,
Love ,it's never ending
Be glad that it is so.

THINK

Not a sound is heard
As in anguish we cry,
Today we are still living,
Tomorrow we may die.

Thinking is realistic,
Maybe pessimistic,
Yes, life is for living,
But not just taking,
Also in the giving.

TRAIN OF LIFE

Life is like a train journey,
Delays, cancellations, strikes,
Is it hit and miss?
Are the signals jammed?
Or are the points just stuck?

Leaves on the line,
Tree down, avalanche,
Running late, or missed,
Life's a bit like that,
Or maybe not…

Will we get there in the end?
We must, we really must,
Even if the line is blocked,
We'll surely get there…
On the bus!

A STUNNING BLACK GOWN

A dress of lace,
A smiling face,
Never a frown,
Remembered, oh so well.
But, truth to tell
Mostly I remember,
The flowing black gown.

A windy day,
Scattering your hair,
But you didn't care
As it blew all around,
And the rain came down.
But still I remember,
The stunning black gown.

Who could forget
The views that surround,
But all I remember,
Is your lovliness,
Dressed to amaze,
Holding my gaze,
In that stunning black gown.

RICH THOUGHTS

Blessed is the morning
That brings the day anew,
Blessed are the flowers,
Bathed in the morning dew.

Blessed is the wakening
To a fresh new day,
Blessed is the peace,
That comes along the way.

Blessed is the freshness
Of a cheerful smile.
Blessed is the one
Who goes the extra mile.

Blessed is the day
That begins with thoughts of you,
And blessed is the evening
Which ends without adieu..

Blessed was your presence,
Blessed was your touch,
Blessed all those happy days,
I miss so very much.

TOMORROW'S DREAM

The gentle smile
Of the sun's first kiss,
The silent breath
Of the morning mist,
As yesterday passes
Into today,
The unknown waits
To stalk its prey.

We stretch and yawn
To greet the day.
Come what may,
It lies in wait,
We know not what,
Or if, or how,
An adventure, or a trial,
Expectations, in denial.

A gentle smile
Or a raging storm,
All uncovered
In another morn,
Sleep is fading
As dawn is breaking,
Yesterday's echo
Is tomorrow's dream.

MOTHER'S DAY

Every day is mothers day,
Not just once a year.
Mothers are so special,
They guard us and protect,
They nurture and they feed us,
And give us lots of love.

Mothers are selfless,
Mothers are unique.
They educate with love,
Cuddle us and play,
Mothers, we all have one,
Love her every day.

MYTHICAL FOREST

Gnarled trees, forgotten dreams,
Lying abandoned, broken,
Tears enough
To fill a stream,
No expression shown,
And seldom spoken.

Mountains of regrets,
Never seen, hidden,
Outside of vision,
A hidden token,
Life has passed,
Somehow unbroken.

Caves of granite, uncovered,
Unknown treasures, lurking
That bid exploring,
Exciting mystery,
Twilight is history,
Seldom seen.

EMPTY SHELL

Life does seem empty,
Nobody to chat
About this, or that.
No one to bring tea,
Or an ice cold drink,
Whilst I'm working
In the garden, in the sun,
Admiring what's been done.

No one to smile,
Or laugh, or tease,
No one to cuddle
Or to please.
Sometimes I'd shout
You'd shout back,
But then a hug
And that was that.

Arguments forgiven,
Then forgotten,
You are missed,
Especially today,
An empty shell,
Of a lifetime spent,
And loved so well.

WHISPERING WIND

Softly sighing on
The wings of the wind,
Whispering through the cornfield,
Rustling leaves above,
Invisible forces around me
To caress the soul with love.

Loneliness, or emptiness,
The wind, somehow it knows.
Talking to me gently,
A force of reassurance
Transports me clear away,
Coming back tomorrow,
But alone again today.

SPECIAL SOMEONE

Sharing life's experiences
With someone whom you love,
Enjoying all on offer
Along life's dusty way,
Like the smell of summer raindrops,
Or the scent of new mown hay.

Sheltering from a hailstorm,
An unexpected thunder crack,
Running down the hillside
The sky turned sudden black,
Then hiding 'neath the branches
Of an aging tree.

Clinging close together
To keep each other warm.
These things, O so simple,
Together became such fun,
Enjoying life together
With you, the special one.

Softly crying at a tragedy
Emotions raw and wide,
Tears you tried to hide,
Till someone made a joke,
Brushed aside then swiftly,
Trying not to choke.

Everyday moments,
Like sheltering from the rain
Or sliding in the snow.
May seem unimportant,
Until that day it comes
And your special someone,
Goes…..

THE TREE

The scented Pine tree,
Tall and strong,
The spreading Chestnut too,
The Willow rustles gently
Then weeps for all to see.

The mighty Oak, a giant
Foreboding, majestic, strong,
King of all the forest,
To whom we bend the knee,
As it towered above us
For many a century.

The Yew, the Ash, the Rowan
In silence they all work,
And slowly clean the air
For human life to be,
As we carry on regardless,
Destroying all we see.

Trees give us shelter
Beauty, and much more,
Holly, Walnut, Beech and Elm
The list goes ever on,
So, go protect a tree.
Better still, go plant one
Or two, or even three.

So to the iconic, historic
Sycamore tree,
Standing in the gap,
For over a century,
With green shoots in defiance
After being slaughtered,
needlessly.

So as man destroys
Pointlessly,
Nature mends
Endlessly.

URBAN HERMIT

I sought a place wherein to dwell
In solitude,
To meditate,
To contemplate,
All life's mystery
And human history,
Throughout time.
To think and reason,
What we are,
And where we go,
Throughout time,
Among the planets,
And the stars,
Jupiter, Saturn, Mars,
To name a few,
Of those we know,
As knowledge grows.

I sought to find somewhere,
To be alone,
Perhaps a cave,
Or hollow tree,
No one to interupt
The thinking,
Of the inner me.
Alas, I soon discovered,
Nature gave me plenty,
Beauty soon uncovered,
No day was ever empty.

Soon I was distracted
By mother nature's charm,
Trees rustling
In summer breeze,
Bird song varied,
And buzzing bees.
Owls that screech
In dead of night,
Foxes calling,
Rabbits rushing,
Badgers digging,
All distracting
From my quest,
To meditate and ponder,
The depth and meaning,
Life and death,
And things of wonder.

The nature and the rising sun,
Thus began to overcome,
I realised, in nature,
You have a friend,
You're not alone,
Distracted easily
By nature's charm.
The Hermit's life
Was not to be,
In cave, or trunk,
Of an old dead tree.
I returned to live,
On an urban street,
With busy people
Who you seldom meet.

Neighbours busied all about,
Unconcerned, and unaware,
They seldom ever notice
The fact you're even there.
Once inside,and doors are shut,
You're left alone,
A Hermits life,
In this urban street,
Where people pass
But seldom greet.

Solitude at last achieved,
Not in the wilderness
As I believed,
But the middle
And the muddle
Of the urban concrete jungle.
To meditate and pray,
Contemplate and think,
Ambition thus achieved,
An urban hermit
At the kitchen sink.

FEEL THE PAIN

Seldom do we appreciate,
What we have
Until it's gone,
And it is no more,
Within life's door,
Till a distant shore,
At the end of time.
We are just mortal,
Nothing lasts forever
Except time,
Eternal time,
Unlike us
Who make a fuss,
And feel betrayed,
When love is lost.
But there is a cost
For happiness.
A worthwhile price,
It's more than nice
Not forever
In this world,
Just on loan.
Merely custodians,
Companions to enjoy,
While we live
Until one dies,
No surprise,
A separation,
Then the pain,
Ahhhh yes..
The pain…

AN EPITAPH

Do not weep now children,
Do not weep for me.
I'm gone into the sunset,
So do not weep for me,
Weep for those still suffering,
Those lacking humility,
Weep for those who hunger,
But do not weep for me.

Weep for the unbelievers,
They have no place to go,
Weep for the lost ones,
But do not weep for me.
Weep for those displaced
And those who suffer pain,
Weep for the homeless,
But do not weep for me.

Weep for those in conflict,
Away from home and family,
Weep now for the cruel ones,
They know not what they do.
But please, do this thing for me,
Think about me kindly, and
although you will not see,
I'll be praying for you,
Daily,
So please, always pray for me.

Printed in Dunstable, United Kingdom